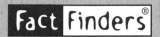

Fact Finders®

CRACKING
THE **MEDIA**
LITERACY
CODE

UNDERSTANDING
$$$
★ ADVERTISING ★

BY EMMA CARLSON BERNE

CONSULTANT:
ROBERT L. MCCONNELL, PHD

CAPSTONE PRESS
a capstone imprint

Fact Finders Books are published by Capstone Press
1710 Roe Crest Drive, North Mankato, Minnesota 56003
www.mycapstone.com

Library of Congress Cataloging-in-Publication Data
Names: Berne, Emma Carlson, author.
Title: Understanding advertising / by Emma Carlson Berne.
Description: North Mankato, Minnesota : Capstone Press, [2019] | Series: Fact finders. Cracking the media
literacy code. | Includes index.
Identifiers: LCCN 2018001959 (print) | LCCN 2018004523 (ebook)
  ISBN 9781543527230 (ebook PDF)
  ISBN 9781543527070 (hardcover)
  ISBN 9781543527155 (paperback)
Subjects: LCSH: Advertising—Juvenile literature.
Classification: LCC HF5829 (ebook) | LCC HF5829 .B475 2019 (print) | DDC 659.1—dc23
LC record available at https://lccn.loc.gov/2018001959

Editorial Credits
Michelle Bisson, editor; Russell Griesmer, designer; Jennifer Bergstrom, production artist; Morgan Walters,
media researcher; Tori Abraham, production specialist

Photo Credits
Alamy: Jeff Morgan 10, left 13, 16, Neil Baylis, right 13, 15, Splash News, 24; Getty Images: Bradenton Herald,
7, Brendan O'Sullivan, 4, VIEW press, 19; Granger, 10; Newscom: National Motor Museum Heritage Images,
14, TELAM Xinhua News Agency, 8, The Print Collector Heritage Images, 11; Shutterstock: Alisara Zilch,
design element throughout, cover, artzenter, 6, balabolka, design element throughout, cover, dnd_project, 27,
Eladora, (head) Cover, Everett Historical, 12, Kaspars Grinvalds, 20, Macrovector, design element throughout,
cover, topform, design element throughout, cover; Wikimedia: Archives New Zealand, 29

Printed in the United States of America.
PA021

TABLE OF CONTENTS

CHAPTER 1

WHERE ARE THE ADS?

You've finished your homework. You've taken out the garbage. Your dad is cooking dinner, and he's said you can get on the laptop for 15 minutes. Yes! You log on to your favorite website. Scroll, scroll, scroll. You laugh at your friend's picture of himself in a scary wig. Then you watch a video someone posted of a baby goat climbing a tree.

You examine a picture of a kid with a new kind of scooter. The scooter has a motor. Do you know this kid, you wonder. Maybe he's in your class. He doesn't look familiar. Wait—what's that? A price? It says the scooter is on special for $65? You sit back in your chair. It was an ad. And you didn't even realize it.

You'll see all kinds of ads when you are on social media.

Advertisers want something specific from you. Public service announcements want you to be aware of a health or safety problem. Political ads want people to vote for a certain politician or cast their ballots a certain way on a political issue. Classified ads might want you to buy a used piano.

Advertising can be manipulative and can contain lies. Advertising can also be genuine and necessary. People need goods and services. Companies provide those things. Advertising helps companies show you their goods and services.

But advertising can also try to send you messages. They might be about you, your friends, your worries, or the person you wish you were. Advertising can sometimes disguise itself as other things. One minute you're watching a scooter video, and the next, you're being sold a scooter.

 manipulate—to change someting in a clever way to influence people to do or think how you want

Ads for food are generally trying to make you hungry!

Ads are everywhere—on billboards by the side of the road, on TV, in magazines and newspapers, and buried in social media feeds. They can run down the sides of email accounts. Ads can be videos on TV or online. They can be photos in magazines, newspapers, or online.

The most straightforward ads show in a direct way what the business wants to sell. This type of ad might explain how a product or service can help the buyer. The advertiser might point out that it is charging less for a product than another company. Now consumers can choose the less expensive product.

All product advertising, no matter how honest, has a goal—to get you to buy what they're selling. An ad might be clever to get your attention, but still be straightforward.

Yet ads can also cross the line into active deception. Sometimes ads pretend to be something else—a TV show, a post from a friend, or a magazine article. Ads might try to make you feel worried or insecure. Only if you buy this product, the ad might imply, can you be well liked.

Sometimes the Internet feels like one big commercial.

Learning to think about ads can help you separate deceptive or unfair advertising from honest advertising.

★ consumer—a person who buys things

★ deception—something that makes people believe what is not true; a lie

★ imply—to suggest rather than say

The video site YouTube advertised a new app to parents in 2015. The site implied the app would help protect young children from bad influences online. The app would let kids more easily find and watch their favorite shows on YouTube. But YouTube mixed in short ads with the shows so the kids would have to see the ads. YouTube put ads on the app that looked like shows—but weren't. Kids had no way of knowing what was an ad and what was a show.

DID YOU KNOW?

Toy companies with products such as LEGO or Mattel often create entire websites for kids. They have games and activities to play online. The websites help them sell their toys.

A website has games for kids but it also has ads.

Adults and kids must become media literate. That means understanding how media works. Then you can learn to take control of ads and their messages. You can examine what the advertiser is trying to send with its message. You can understand to whom the messages are aimed.

With your new knowledge, you can decide for yourself if you want or need the goods or services being offered through the ad. And you can protect yourself against deceptive ads.

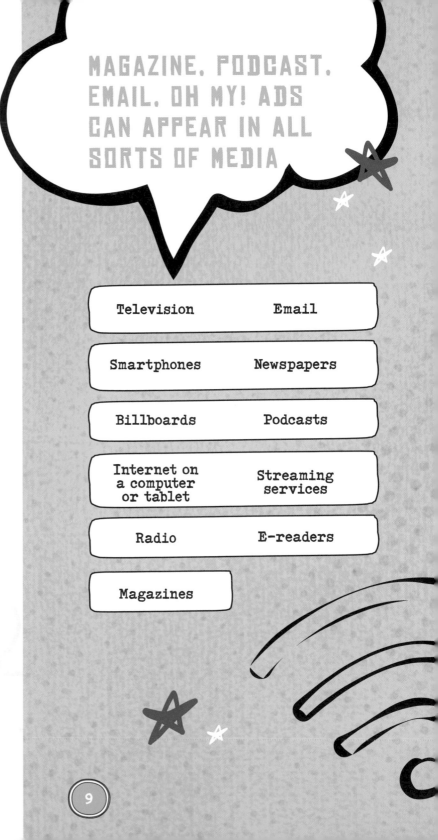

MAGAZINE. PODCAST. EMAIL. OH MY! ADS CAN APPEAR IN ALL SORTS OF MEDIA

Television	Email
Smartphones	Newspapers
Billboards	Podcasts
Internet on a computer or tablet	Streaming services
Radio	E-readers
Magazines	

CHAPTER 2

300 YEARS OF ADVERTISING

Advertising has existed since civilization's earliest days. Street vendors shouted out their goods. Shop owners posted pictures of the food they sold for those who couldn't read. Others tacked flyers to the sides of buildings. In Colonial America, newspapers often contained advertisements. Early ads announced the departures of ships that were soon to sail and were ready to take on passengers. People also ran ads about household goods they wanted to sell or stolen goods they wanted to find.

Ads for ship departures were printed in a 1749 newspaper.

A more disturbing form of an early ad was the announcement that someone had enslaved people to sell. Some ads were looking for those who had run away. Until slavery ended in the United States in 1865, enslaved people were treated as if they were products. Like products, this meant black people could be bought and sold.

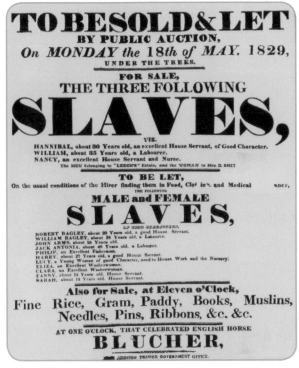

Ads announcing the sale of enslaved people were common from colonial times until the Civil War ended slavery in the U.S.

Advertisements in early newspapers were not illustrated. They were printed in the same kind of type that was used for news stories. Often they were either placed in the regular newspaper columns or put in the back of the paper.

Mass production changed the world as we know it.
It helped advertising grow as a business.

By the middle of the 19th century, mass-produced goods were available to many people. Before this time, most things were not mass-produced. That meant there was little use for advertisements that would spread the name of the company and its products to a larger audience. That changed once companies had many products they wanted to distribute, such as cars or machine-made clothing.

During the early 1900s, the technology needed to print colorful illustrations in magazines and newspapers became more common. Companies could then print attractive ads selling lotions, powders, saddles, and canned food.

Stores like Sears printed huge catalogs advertising everything you could think to order—even kits that contained all the materials needed to build a house.

Advertisements often focused on people's worries. "Worried about smelling bad?" an ad might ask. "Try Odorono," one of the first women's deodorants.

Do you want to be as lovely and rich as this elegant woman in a dinner gown? Well, she uses Pond's Vanishing Cream.

 mass-produce—to produce in quantity, usually with a machine

 distribute—to give out or deliver, especially to members of a group

Ads have been produced by agencies in the U.S. as early as the 19th century. Companies hire agencies to create ads for their products that are interesting, creative, funny, or even scary. Usually, the ads are aimed at specific groups of people. The targets might be women who work in the home

In the 1950s cars were advertised as luxury items.

and have more than one child, for instance. Or they might target teenagers or men who live in rural areas. Many of the agencies are located on Madison Avenue in New York City. This led to the entire industry being nicknamed "Madison Avenue." The Madison Avenue agencies revolutionized advertising.

Many ads resembled tiny works of art. Sometimes they tried to surprise or shock the viewer. In 1959 an ad agency created an ad for the Volkswagen Beetle that was the opposite of most car ads of that era. Car ads usually showed a big, colorful car full of smiling people, often driving in a beautiful landscape. The ad would often describe the car as fast, big, and fancy. The Beetle ad showed a tiny black car on an empty white background. "Think Small," the headline read. Underneath, the ad told viewers that Volkswagens were small, slow, and simple. They were everything cars were not supposed to be at a time when bigger was better. The ad surprised viewers. It made them laugh—and remember the Beetle. More importantly, the ad got people to buy the little car.

The only water a Volkswagen needs is the water you wash it with.

Ads for the Volkswagen Beetle changed the advertising world. Suddenly, humor was in.

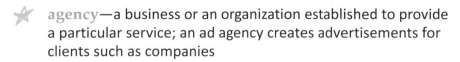 agency—a business or an organization established to provide a particular service; an ad agency creates advertisements for clients such as companies

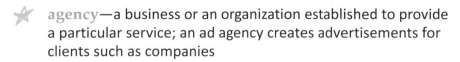 revolutionize—to change greatly or completely

Creative or straight, funny or serious, product advertisements have always tried to achieve the same goal. They aim to sell things to consumers, even if that means stretching the truth.

Patent Medicines: Advertising Pioneers

Many people used **patent medicines** during the 19th century. Manufacturers put all kinds of ingredients in mixtures and then made wild claims about their usefulness.

The manufacturers attracted readers' attention with bold letters and attractive pictures of animals, children, and pretty women. The ads claimed that the medicine could cure different illnesses. None of these claims were true. But the government didn't **regulate** what it said at that time, so it was perfectly legal.

Patent medicine manufacturers offered free samples, put their ads on billboards, and mailed ads directly to consumers. All of the methods were new advertising tools. Many people believed the claims. For some, the products had no effects. For others, the effects were worse than what they'd tried to cure.

 patent medicine—a product, marketed as medicine, available for sale without a doctor's prescription; it has contents of unproven effectiveness

 regulate—make rules that businesses must follow

CHAPTER 3

WHAT DO ADS DO?

The world of Internet-based advertising has only been around since the mid-1990s. It opened doors for advertisers that never existed before. Ads are everywhere online. The feeds of social media sites like Facebook and Snapchat have ads sandwiched in between posts from people. When a user tries to read an article online, a pop-up ad often appears first. You have to wait a few seconds, then click the ad closed to read the text you were trying to see.

Online ads are doing the same thing product ads have always tried to do. They are trying to sell you goods and services. So what's the big deal? The ads can be aimed specifically at you and what you like. Companies have paid to place products in movies and TV shows for many years. For example, a character might drink a Coke with the logo turned toward the camera.

If you see an ad like this in your online feed, it may be because Facebook knows you love computers.

But now, when people put their preferences into a profile on Facebook, for instance, Facebook can tell which ads might attract them. Someone might say in a profile that he or she likes music. So Facebook might show the person ads from a business that sells concert tickets. If someone is into fashion, Facebook might show him or her ads for stylish shoes.

Much of users' online information is connected and available to advertisers. That includes social media, websites, and email.

Bloggers with large followings can earn money from advertisers.

Blogging is another new area for advertisers. Bloggers write about topics of interest to them and their readers. But you might not know that companies sometimes pay bloggers to write about their products in a positive way. A blogger who writes about power tools, for instance, might tell how he cut down a tree at his house. He might add that he used a certain brand of chainsaw and was pleased with how it worked. He might even put a link to the tool company's website in his post.

The blogger is required by law to state on his website if he has been paid by the tool company. Have you ever read such a statement? Probably not. These statements are generally found at the bottom of the web page in teensy type.

The places that advertising appears have changed dramatically since the 1920s. But the messages that ads try to convey have remained the same. Ads have always focused on people's fears, hopes and dreams.

Do you want to be popular? Do you want to be like the other kids? Are you afraid of being bullied or excluded? An ad might imply that if you have the newest and best LEGO sets, like the cool kids in your school, then you will be popular. The ad might show children dressed in bright, fashionable clothes clustered around a LEGO set on the floor. They are all laughing and playing. They like each other and they're having fun. If you get these LEGO sets, the ad implies, then you might be more like these kids.

A billboard ad for Disneyland literally appeared in the sky. The plane was covered with Disneyland characters. Of course, passengers couldn't see it once they were on the plane but they could see it from inside the terminal. And on the runway. And on billboards by the side of the road. Even if a person hadn't wanted to go to Disneyland before, chances are that seeing that ad would make you want to go. And, advertisers were hoping, you'd want to fly there on the airline that created the ad.

DID YOU KNOW?

Most models weigh about 23 percent less than the average woman. That's about one-quarter less of body weight. Ads promoting dieting have made a lot of money. It is estimated that companies that promote diet aids bring in $33 billion a year, every year, in the United States. Meanwhile, more and more girls, boys, and even grown-ups have trouble eating a healthy diet because they are so afraid of gaining weight.

Can advertisers simply say or do anything they want in an ad? And can they advertise products that they know are harmful? Can advertisers show people in a way that is not accurate? For example, saying cigarettes are good for your health? That's something advertisers really did in the past.

The U.S. Constitution protects the right of people to speak and write freely and to have a free press. Our economy depends on people's ability to buy and sell goods freely. But the government has to protect its citizens against danger. That includes protecting against false advertising or ads that encourage violence or **prejudice** against certain people or groups. The Federal Trade Commission (FTC) is the government body in charge of overseeing advertising.

The U.S. has rules so advertisers can't lie in their ads. If they do, they can be fined and forced to remove the ad or change it. The government also has rules about advertising harmful products. Until 1997 a cartoon character called Joe Camel was used to sell Camel-brand cigarettes. The FTC filed a complaint against the maker of Camel cigarettes. It said that the company was promoting its dangerous product to children. The company fought the case but eventually stopped using Joe Camel to sell its cigarettes.

prejudice—an opinion about others that is unfair or not based on facts

Many roadside billboards have public service announcements.

Ads can get a brief message across in a powerful way. Public service announcements (PSAs) are a type of advertisement that does not seek to sell anything. Instead, PSAs try to spread a general, useful message to the public. The ads may be about many things. Some of the most common include ads about the dangers of smoking, drinking and driving, and gambling.

Political ads often show up on TV, online, and in mailings. The ads often try to encourage voters to pick one candidate over another. They might use bright colors and big bold letters. They tell voters the positive things their candidate has done and promises to do.

Campaign ads can be negative too. Sometimes called attack ads, they often use dark, muddy colors, black-and-white pictures, and scary lettering. They describe the opposing candidate as dangerous or bad.

DID YOU KNOW?

When people download apps onto their phones or tablets, the makers of the apps get access to information. They can find out about a person's likes, dislikes, and ways of living. Then the makers of the apps can target ads that will appeal to that person. The ads will show up in the apps. It's called "in-app" advertising.

CHAPTER 4

THE FUTURE: ADVERTISING JUST FOR YOU

As the world becomes more and more connected online, advertisers will have access to more and more data about consumers' likes and dislikes. After googling "Nerf blaster," for example, users will see pictures of Nerf blasters on their social media accounts and in their email programs.

It's possible that ads will be able to interact with smart watches in the future. A person might experience an ad not just by gazing at it but by living it through virtual reality technology. Online ads and even TV commercials might be tailored specifically to each person. The ads would be based on what each person might have eaten, bought, and done recently. And advertisers could track all of it.

But people can be in control of ads rather than the other way around. How? First, be aware of which content is an ad. Look closely at the words on each game, article, story, or video you click on.

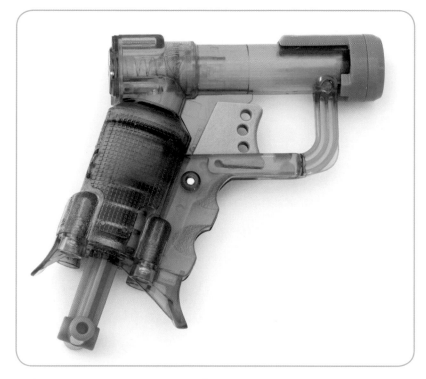

Google something like "dart gun blaster" and you will begin to see ads for them everywhere online.

Look for words such as "sponsored," "ad," "advertisement," or "this is an advertisement." They may be in small letters at the top or bottom or on the sides of the ad. Look for brand names anywhere in the ad. One example might be a game in which a bunny hops through a meadow made of LEGO bricks.

Product ads often have words that encourage consumers to interact with them. They include "download now," or "buy now," or "watch a demo." If you are using a web browser, look carefully at the web address. Commercial sites end in .com (for "company") and are probably trying to sell you something.

There are places on the Internet that are free from ads. School sites, ebook sites, and school-approved databases usually do not have ads. They are generally safe places to visit. Other sites that typically don't show ads are government or nonprofit organization sites. They usually end in .gov or .org.

When you see a product ad, ask yourself how the ad makes you feel. Excited? Fearful? Ashamed? What image of you is the ad trying to project? Is the ad making promises about what will happen to you if you buy the product? Or does it make threats about what might happen if you don't?

Examine ads with a critical eye. That way, you can make solid choices about whether that product is right for you. People need safe, reliable, interesting products. And manufacturers have to be able to tell us about them through advertising.

As consumers, we need to be able to recognize ads that stretch the truth. We also need to be able to recognize ads that try to get us to buy by tricking us. By increasing your media literacy, you can become a wiser, more confident consumer.

Government sites often show PSAs such as this one. These ads encourage us to eat a healthy diet.

GLOSSARY

agency (AY-juhn-see)—a business or an organization established to provide a particular service; an ad agency creates advertisements for clients such as companies

consumer (kuhn-SOO-muhr)—a person who buys things

deception (di-SEP-shen)—something that makes people believe what is not true; a lie

distribute (dis-TRIB-yute)—to give out or deliver, especially to members of a group

imply (IM-pli)—to suggest rather than say

manipulate (muh-NIP-yuh-late)—to change someting in a clever way to influence people to do or think how you want

mass-produce (Mas-PRA-dyus)—to produce in quantity, usually with a machine

patent medicine (PAT-ent MED-i-cin)—a product, marketed as medicine, available for sale without a doctor's prescription; it has contents of unproven effectiveness

prejudice (PREJ-uh-diss)—an opinion about others that is unfair or not based on facts

regulate (REG-yu-late)—to make rules that businesses must follow

revolutionize (REV-e-lu-sha-nize)—to change greatly or completely